BROKEN FLOWERS

AND OTHER STAIRWAYS TO HEAVEN

Other Books by Robert M. Drake

Spaceship (2012)

Science (2013)

Beautiful Chaos (2014)

Black Butterfly (2015)

A Brilliant Madness (2015)

Broken Flowers (2016)

Gravity (2017)

Moon Theory (2017)

Young And Rebellious (2018)

Chasing The Gloom (2018)

For Excerpts and Updates please follow:

Instagram.com/rmdrk
Facebook.com/rmdrk
Twitter.com/rmdrk

ISBN: 978-0-9862627-9-1

Book Cover: Robert M. Drake

Cover Image licensed by Shutter Stock Inc.

ATTENTION: SCHOOLS AND BUSINESSES

Robert M. Drake books are available at quantity discounts with bulk purchase for educational, business, or sales promotional use. For information, please e-mail:
rmdrkone@gmail.com

For Sevyn,

It has been a pleasure meeting you in this life.

It brings me joy knowing that you have found me. Just remember, when you're a woman, remember to read these words, and know that most, if not all, were inspired by you.

I love you. I love you. I love you.

Thank you for giving me peace.

This book will not contain any images.

This time you will have to draw them all in your head.

CONTENTS

BROKEN FLOWERS

AND OTHER STAIRWAYS TO HEAVEN

ROBERT M. DRAKE

Go On

And you will go on
searching for the best of you
and you will never find it,
but that is the point.

Do not miss the point.

Missing it will make
the beautiful struggle useless.

And believe me you need it.

It is what will make you.

The fact that you will keep
trying to find the perfect you,
the perfect moment
and connection and love.

And you will die trying.

We will all die trying.

But that is the goddamn point.

To never stop searching for
the things that remind you

how to feel, how to live
and how to die the right way,
your way . . .

The only way to do things.

Do Not Run from Yourself

You can run all you want
but one day
someone is going to take
a hold of you, kid,
and find you
and maybe they will even
run with you.

And who knows
Maybe they will stick around
for longer than usual
and make things harder
to run away from.

We are all running away
or toward something, kid,
Let us just hope whatever
it is we crash into does not
make the day dimmer
and the night darker.

You deserve at least
ten thousand suns.

We all do.

When My Brother Left

Brother,
I remember when you told me
you felt different
and at that moment
I couldn't understand why.

A few years later
and now I, too, feel different,
like the first time I heard that one song—
the one that changed my life.

I now understand
what you were going through.

I get it.

I met a girl on a train
and now I feel different about
almost everything,
and I want to go back to the way
things were, but things
are not that easy when you are
in love.

Things just never look the same.

Sometimes I drown things, people
and memories. Sometimes I rise
to the surface and kiss the shore
and sometimes you are the ocean.

I Miss You

You seemed fine
the last time we spoke.

You seemed better,
as if somewhere in this
endless dark space
you found a map,
and it led you
out of this world.

I hope you find what
you're looking for.

I hope you come back soon.

Tonight It Is Good

Life is harder when you
see it for what it is,
for what it can be.

From bad to worse,
from worse to better.
And the night becomes day,
and the pain becomes less
than of what it was
the night before.

Tonight it is all good.

The company is all good
and none of us worry about
the morning sun.

Tonight all the people have
a flower somewhere inside
of them, and they are looking
for somewhere to bloom.

Somewhere to be themselves
in the middle of the night.

What Is Important

What you consider important right now
might change within the next moment.

You could never be content
considering everything is always changing
and growing.

The same with people.

They are always changing and growing.
You have to learn how to change
and grow with them
if you ever want a shot at someone to love.

Even if that means leaving
the things you are familiar with
behind.

I Wish I Saw You

I'm losing parts of myself
that I haven't found yet,
and I can feel them
walking in and out of me.

Some never return
and some come back,
just to fuck with me.

You know that feeling?
Two people slowly becoming strangers,
slowly burning till there's nothing left?

That's what this is like
and I think I'm okay with that.

Maybe in some distant future,
in another place,
or even in another earth,
you and I could be more
than just people we used to know.

I do not know how it began
but I do remember how it ended
and I will find you in the
endless days of summer because
that was where I fell into you.

What You Became

You are all
the old records I listen to.

You are the books I read,
all the places I visit,
and all the poetry I have yet to write.

My dearest friend . . .

You are the forgiveness
I need to give myself
for not being there for you.

You are more than these
words and these feelings
you have left behind.

You are light,
and the light contained inside of you,
it is beyond belief,
the theory of everything.

What Some People Bring

Someone will always
be watching you.

Someone will always be
out to get you,
no matter where you go.

You cannot run far enough
from the bullshit
people bring.

You will find people
like this everywhere.

They are so damn sad
about their own lives
that they feel the need
to bring others down.

You go on . . .
Someone will always be
there, you will see,
and you must, for the goodness
of your own life . . .

Watch back with eyes
like the moon and blood
in your hands.

Watch back and wait
for one of them to make
their move.

Where You Can Find Me

And I will wait for you
under the soft rain.

I will wait for you
in the empty bottles of wine,
in the ripped sky,
and in the moments
where I picked myself up.

I will wait for you
where I first met you.

I will wait for you here,
because this was the place
where we saw each other
for the last time.

We Get It

Yeah you are real, we get it.

You remind the crowd around you
every five minutes.

You talk about
how much alcohol you drink,
every five minutes.

You talk about
how many women you sleep with,
every five minutes.

You talk about this and that,
things that you think appeal to the crowd.

We get it! We get it! God we get it!

You are as real as they come,
but you know what type of person
does not have to say they are
"a real motherfucker"?

A *REAL* motherfucker.

It is raining again on my side
and I cannot help but to wonder
if you are safe and sound. I am
sorry for all the storms I left
behind.

Glory

You only go to that place
when you feel like
you don't fit in,
when you think people
do not understand you.

You only go to that place
when you want to be alone
because you think
the world wants to rob you
of your glory.

But that might not be the case.
That might not even be
what you need.

So do not go there,
that place is not for you.
Do not go away, you might
lose yourself in there
and you might never find
your way back.

The Sun Wants to Come In

You never really see
how bad it can get
until you become
a part of the problem
and it usually happens
without us even knowing it.

And most will never know,
that's how it is.

People, almost all are
always quicker
to fall into any problem
at any given moment.

It is almost like they follow
us and they are waiting
for a little sunshine to enter
us through our eyes.

And that is when they strike.

They overflow and dry
the sun out like a lit match
interested in the water.

15

This dark cloud is easy
to follow, it is hard to escape,
but that is our problem.

And that is one we must
learn to starve on our own.

No One Wants to Stay

Sometimes I feel like
I have been here too long,
maybe even forever.

I feel like I am trapped in this page.

Caged inside myself.

Trapped beneath the ground
looking for the photons
that will lead me out,
that will leak me out,
and keep me out.

no one ever wants to stay
in the same place
or do the same things
for several years.

The years begin to look
the same and everything
that is the same becomes
madness, becomes hysterical,
if you stare long enough.

Now tell me how sad
it is to have so much poetry inside

but not enough pages,
not enough words
to write them down.

That is what this is like,
like all the love I have for you
trapped inside my body.

All the nights I envision you,
together with our hands mangled.

That is what this is like,
like the everything
and the nothing about you
is inside of me
and I do not know what
to do or where to go.

sometimes I want to show
you more of me,
but I do not know how.

You should talk to strangers
more. You should learn from them
and grow with them. Sometimes
a stranger could save you and
sometimes a smile could change
a life.

Speak to Me

I always found myself
getting into the hardest of situations,
in and out of the worst
moments or so I thought,
but that's how I was. I was reckless.

I was always willing to go
through hell and back
as long as it meant something.

And I was never sure
what it meant to begin with,
but if it spoke to me beyond the words,
beyond the flesh,
then I went for it, in that very moment.

I went for it blindly
whether it was good or bad.

I dove my ambition, my inspiration,
into these rare little moments
like a giant rock
falling from the sky.

Wood Tavern

It's been a while since
I last went out,
perhaps too long,
or long enough for me
to dream of crowds.

Sometimes you just have to
go out there and experience
life a little. You can't always stay
in and expect to learn
something new about people
from reading goddamn books.

Human understanding
does not work that way.

I go into Wood Tavern one night
and of course it is a rare thing
for me to see this haven empty.
"There are too many people." I thought.

Too many faces and they are waiting
for something—like a spaceship.
Something to come out of the sky
and tell them how beautiful they are.

And they are, every single one of them.

It felt good to be out.

I walked to the bar
and I got a drink spilled on me.

This is how good turns bad.

The girl turns around and says
"Sorry." then turns back around
and goes on with her night.

Now my shirt was wet, but
I went on with my night too.
I drank, I laughed, and I forgot
how I left.

When I got home I sat in front of the
old typewriter and wrote this here prose
you are reading right now . . .

I typed and thought,

I thought and typed

and I still do not understand
humans at all, including myself.

You Are My Air

I hope you see things
differently now,

and I hope you know
we did not destroy ourselves
when we thought our

worlds had ended.

Because we are still here
and we still exist
because the other still lives.

You are my air

and I am your lungs.

"there are lights in the sky,"
said the little girl.
"Those are not lights dear,
those are people," said her
father.

I Want To Save You

I told you I wanted to
save the world,

to do something about
all this pain.

You told me how that
was impossible and how
I am only one person.

Nothing is impossible.

It takes one sun to light the sky,
one moon to move the tide,
and one love to change a life.

I love you.

I will change you.

I will save us all.

Closer Than We Think

I feel the same way.

You feel the same way.

Everyone feels the same way.

And we just do not know
how to tell each other.

We just want a way
out of our own humanity,
out of our own skin.

Because the world has made us believe
we are not beautiful,
how we are not capable
of becoming art.

But I see you walking.

I see the paint falling off
your shoes as if
I see Van Gogh,
Michelangelo, and Da Vinci
pouring out of the way
you move.

You are beautiful,
and the world wants to
mutilate your story.

It wants to erase the words
so we all think the same.
So we all think less.
I need you to know you are
more.

You have to see it.
Open your eyes.

Before It Began

And just like that,
before it even began
it was over.

The moment I thought
I belonged,
I found myself
back where I started.

And I thought
"How in the hell could
anyone keep their sanity
playing this game?"

And that answer was simple:

"We were all willing to
die a little for a chance
to be loved."

The Love In You

But you have to find the
place that brings out
the human in you.

The soul in you.
The love in you.

You have to sing a little
in there.

You do not have to do it
all the time,
but at least every once
in a while.

Anything beats the silence.

Anything beats
the quietness of the clock
when you are missing
the company of another

person.

The child in you did not die.
The child in you is alive
and it is waiting to show you
the world in a different light.

When You Cross My Mind

Sometimes
I think of you,
and sometimes
I wonder if you made it
out of your life alive.

I know it is not safe
to stay within yourself.

For almost all
who have ever found
something deep enough
to stir them,
have found it out
of their goddamn
normal lives.

And I am still here,
looking for you
on the other side.

Strange Beautiful Girl

There is something
strange about your beauty.

The way your eyes clash,
they make me feel
as if you are from
another time,
perhaps even
another planet,
another moment.

One that defeats what I am,
and one that defines me
to the raw bone.

What I am trying to say is,
you break me down
in ways I could have
never imagined.

We Can Still Fly

There will always be
parts of me that only you
can unlock,
that only you can
come back to save
and that only you can
calm, too soon.

What remains of me,
will always fill
the emptiness in you.
It will always complete
all that we have.

The only parts
we have not learned
to say good-bye to.

The only parts
where we

can still be free.

I Will Return

And if you ever came back
then I'd promise
to give you the raw truth,
and how it was all about
me when I left you.

You weren't ready,
and I wasn't either.

I was somewhere else.

I was looking for ways
to better myself, to heal.

And you were stuck
on the past, believing
it would somehow save
us from our future.

I couldn't give in.

I'm sorry.

I am better than that.

Tigers and Women

Some women are more
dangerous than tigers,
and having at least one
on your side might be
the smartest thing
a man can do.

But treat them well,
for all things change overnight.

If you push them a little
they can become something else,
something like a killer
and their genius is enough
to send a man into suicide,
into hell.

It is true . . .

A woman can turn a man
against himself
and there is nothing more
deadly than that.

If your breath tells your story
then let it flow with the wind.
let it touch the sky and make
love to the moon. I want to feel
you everywhere I go.

The Freedom You Deserve

I'd like to believe
that maybe somewhere,
out there, in the vast darkness,
you have finally found
that freedom you would
always talk about.

And I'd like to believe
that you are a bird
and I am the wind
that pushes you
toward the sun.

And that maybe
the light in you did not
burn out, that maybe
it just left for a little while
and that maybe one day
it will soon find its
way back home.

I Don't Know You Anymore

We are all fighting
to be ourselves
in a world that tells us
who we should be.

And it makes me wonder
if I am in love
with the real you
or just the person you
think you are.

What We Have Inside

Sitting here,
next to you,
I have come
to the conclusion
how it is all the same.

From stars to people,
we are all
drowning
in a pool
filled with too much
to handle.

Too much stress.

Too much fear.

It rises like the vapor
that escapes from our
lungs and bursts into
nothing, into air.

It is all the same,
and it all ends the same.

From stars to people.

We die within ourselves,
waiting for whatever it is
our souls are made of
to claim us and soften
us up to drift away
into the sky.

Sitting here,
next to you,
I have come to the
conclusion,
how it is all the same.

From stars to people,
we are all
struggling with parts
of ourselves
we are too afraid
to reveal.

Feel It in Your Lungs

Look up at the sky.

This must be the sign.

The one we look for
to get away.

The one we look for
when such sad things happen.

If there is something you
have been waiting for,
then this is it.

You feel that air filling your lungs?

That is it . . .

Today . . .

can still be yours.

I made myself from all the love
you never gave me, from all the
attention I never received.
I am strong now and I do not need
you.

Then There Is You

What you gave me
only happens once
and it is not meant
to come back again.

So if I must put it into words
then I must admit,
how not all good things are good
and not all bad things are bad.

And then there is you
and you really fucked me over,
but it felt good,
at least good enough.

And I cannot understand why,
but you still pull out the laughter
in me.

You are in my head
when no one else is around.

It Slip through Your Hands

You took someone
that understood you:

a lover or a friend.
And you watched them
become the only thing
worth clinging to
in the brokenness of the world.
And then, it ends,
as all things end,
suddenly and fast.

Like one day you are
shaped by their laughter,
and then the next day,
eaten alive by their memory.
I can't understand it at all.

You build yourself with
someone you love
and in an instant they are gone.

It ends,
and all you are left with
is

the bitterness
that made sense
in the company
of what
once was.

Love will always be
one of those things,
and it will always hurt
a little more than the last time.

You cannot get away from it
and
that is all
that is needed
to say
about that.

Do What You Must

Anything could happen here.

Maybe you will find someone
and fall in love.

But of course,
just like everyone else,
you keep spending most of your time
looking.

And you have been looking
hard enough, so hard
that when it finally arrives,
you barely remember what it was
you were looking for
and
when it comes to you
it usually arrives beyond the expectation.

And you,
like the person you never knew,
ignore it.

It comes close enough,
and it is all too fast to hold.

No matter how far you go.
I will always be near. I will
always be with you, even when
you feel alone.

And then you,
like the person you never knew,
you do nothing,
you say nothing,

and think nothing . . .

as you watch the love of your life
pass you by.

I Remember You

You look different now,
like someone else
and you sound
like someone else too.

And I can barely recognize you anymore.
But there is something
familiar inside of you,
that chaos,
that same wild energy
that I have.

And tonight I see it piercing
out of you,
and it is calling my name,
the same way mine called yours
many moons ago,
like the night I betrayed myself
and fell fast
into love.

I Miss You Again

If I told you
I did not miss you
then I am a liar.

I miss you.

I miss you.

I miss you.

But you have become
another stranger,
someone I used to know.

Another sunset
with no other place to go.

Give Yourself a Chance

Too many faces,
too many places,
many things within many things
and in so many ways
they could all inspire your life,
if only
you gave them all
a chance.

Let me put it like this, in one hundreds years we will all be dead. so why not express what we feel while we are still here.

Dualism

There is a sun to your moon.
A soul to your body.

A yes to your no.

You are alive while you are dying.

Sleeping while you are awake.

There is a God to your devil.

A dream to your nightmare.

It can go on. It will always go on.

There is a forever to your end.

A friend to your stranger.

A movement to your stillness.

A hello to your last good-bye.

A yesterday to your today.

A past to your present.

A wholeness to your emptiness.

A love to your hate.

A something to your nothing.

But most of all,
there is a happiness to your sadness.

And if you ever lose it, just remember,
soon enough it will find you
and the ride back
will be the most precious thing
known to your earth.

This Mad Cycle

And like everything
that matters—it goes on,
and then it is ignored,
and then it is left to be forgotten.

And it never stops,
this cycle,
this endless war
of attention and appreciation.
It greets no end.

It is all, taken from
the people we see every day,
the places,
and all things that pass us by.

It is all taken for granted, eventually.

It all goes on.

What to Do if I Break

Catch me now
as I break
into a million pieces.

Into the air,
into the ocean,
and into all the fiery regions
where people like us
fight for a chance
to be loved.

Rooms and Memory

I am here
because you
made me up in your head.

I am here
because it is easier
to echo through the rooms
in your mind
than the rooms we try
to each other in at night.

I am here.

I am all around you,
inside, staying.

I am in your head.

Keep me in there
and I will always be around.

I will always be near,
even when you feel
like you need to get away.

You should follow your heart.
It does not always get you into
trouble, for sometimes the heart
finds what the eye cannot see,
and believe me, there is so much
of it around you.

Real Is Real

What is wrong with the world?

We used to hate racism, violence,
poverty, famine, and more.

Now everyone hates on anything,
anytime they get the chance to.

The music you listen to.

The films you watch.

The books you read.

The clothes you wear
and the way you speak.

They even hate you in your own skin.

If you tripped over,
they would even hate on
the way you fell.

The real of the real is,

how people do not know
what to hate on anymore.

51

They have all ran out of things to destroy.

Unravel

Unravel this skin, what it is
that holds me together,
what it is that contains all the pieces of me.

Unravel me, save me, and set me free
in the silence of all things that go on to be
ignored.

Unravel me, in the train, on a Sunday
afternoon,
in the middle of the rain,
or when there is nothing left to do.
Unravel me and find me,
beneath the skin, where the chaos that
makes me is beautiful.

Unravel me to understand me.

I will wait there. I will rest there.

And you will learn to love me there.

A Bird Flew Through

I'd like to believe that
somewhere out there
someone has done the right
thing with you.

I'd like to believe
that someone has made you laugh
in the middle of the night,
that someone has left the sun
in your pocket, in your hair and
in those little moments where
you feel free.

I'd like to believe that
you are flying within yourself
because there is a paradise in you.

There is so much more.

And
I hope you are doing well,
even if it is not with me.

I do not know why people hurt but
I do know one thing, silence heals
everything and I have enough of
it to save the world.

And Here We Are

And here we are,
two people pretending to be
people we are not,
two people wanting to be more.

So when we tell other people
we used to know each other,
it's just us saying:

We once knew people
we could have been,
and
maybe when all of this
suffering is over I'll see you
again and build something
real and be happy there.

I Built Cathedrals out of You

I know I do not
know you anymore
but
you still remind me
of what it was like
to be here,
to be in peace.

You will always be
the best parts to all
the forgotten places
I used to love.

What We Are

It is not about the places
you have seen
or the things you own.

It is about the people
you have met and the way
they made you feel.

So pick and choose.

You do not need all of them
to make it through the day,
just a few,
and there are always a few
good people coming in
and out of your life.

So please do not be afraid.

Keep their trust.

Their friendship is important.

Another Earth

I am not from this earth.

I cannot cope with the ways
of the world:

It is too damn hard.

Where I am from,
there are no photos to scroll,
no videos to watch,
no small bright screens
and no buttons to type
what I am thinking.

Where I am from,
we wonder what people
are up to, go see them,
and sit outside with them
for hours.

I do not know where it
went wrong and I do not know
how to fix it.

What I am trying to say is,
I miss the old you,
the real you,

and I want to forget
what we have become,
what this world has become.

And I hope we see each other soon.

I have so much to tell you.

There is darkness trapped in your
ribcage and there is also light.
What you do with the two is up to
you. I just hope you do not confuse
the two. The world needs night
and day to function and so do you.

Go Outside

When someone smiles at you
for no reason.

When you are inside a room
filled with people you love.

When a miracle happens.

When your best friend says good-bye.

When you leave that city that changed your
life.

When you're on a train and you fall in love
with a stranger.

When you pluck a flower
and ignore it has a few hours to live.

When you lie in your bed
and think about the night before.

When you take a photo with someone
you will never see again.

When your heart is broken
and slowly heals itself.

When you lose yourself in the chaos
of the world,
to find yourself in the end.

This is where you hurt the most.

This is where you live the most.

In the moments that give you breath,
and in the moments that take it away.

Filled In-boxes

"R. M. Drake, your work is too long now.
I liked you better when you wrote short
things for me to read."

"R. M. Drake, you have changed.
Your style is too different and difficult to
swallow now."

"R. M. Drake, I miss the old you.
You used to be so much better."

These are the kind of messages I get now.

Hell, I guess I'm not supposed to grow and
evolve.

I guess I am supposed to be inhuman and
not learn a thing as time goes on.

Silly humans must learn.

If you are not changing then you are not
growing and if you are not growing then
there is no chance of survival.

Surviving is the rebellion against oneself.

It is the change that happens even if we do
not want it to arrive ourselves.

Real Talk

Cause love is real
and talk is cheap
and you had enough words
to bring down
the whole goddamn city.

And I, like the fool,
believe in them
and that is probably
the only thing real between us.

You got me
and I got words
and every single one of them
drunk in the lie of love.

And it is not enough to say,
you fucked me over.

You fucked me over like
all lovers who get fucked over.

They take it all in,
and exhale,
while trying to figure out
where all the love is really
meant to go.

Wild girl with wild hair, I see you
and I know what you are up to. You
want the world and everything in it
and there is nothing, anyone could do
to stop you. Just Remember, a tamed
woman will never leave her mark on
the world. Stay wild.

Violent Power

Power and violence,
now they must go hand in hand.

But c'mon no one ever talks about it
and when they do,
people act like they know about it,
but the truth is,
nobody knows anything about it.

Not even the ones starting
the goddamn wars know
anything about it.

And there they go wanting more power
and then think they will gain it
by killing each other.

But that is not true power.

There is no true force in violence.

The times are changing.

If any of you reading this wants power,
then inspire someone with all heart
and do not pretend.

Go in all the way.

Believe in their goodness,
believe,
the same way a child would believe.

Even the worst of wars are won
by those who believe in something
greater than themselves.

The Generation

I cannot help but wonder
how some people
have the power to do anything in the world:

save it, cure it, and change it,
but go on to destroy it themselves.

They destroy it as if it is the only thing they
can do.

This generation has it all wrong.
They use fear to lead
and violence to control.

They are fed lies
and do not know what to believe
in anymore.

They do not know each other
and they do not know where to go.

This Reality

We are in fact a part
of this prison but often
my comrades and I would say,
if ever we were to escape
this reality, this prison,
we would find ourselves
in a bigger prison, in a bigger reality,
and so on and so forth.

So even if we wanted to,
we could never be free,
for there will always be
something bigger,
something better,
and something harder
to run away from.

Just like you,

there will always be a bigger
and better person
within the person,

of the person that you are.

Do not become like other people.
People are full of shit and they
are mostly wrong. Trust yourself
only you know how to fill your
lungs with breath. Only you know
who you are.

The Sun Is Like You

And everything seems
to feel better
when you are around,
and now I see this light
and it kind of lets me see
where I am going.

I now know where I have to go.

I will tell you when I get there.

I will send mail to you
with all the little things
that will remind me of you.

For Gui

And all I want is to bring you back
from the dead,

my brother.

And all I want is to tell your mother
how everything will be okay.

And all I want is to wake up
and let this all be some kind of terrible joke.

And all I want is to forget that last time
I told you good-bye.

And all I want is one more day with you,

for I know I could have saved you from that
last night you spent on earth.

And all I want is tell you

I am sorry for not being a friend.

I'm sorry.
I'm sorry.
I'm sorry.

That is all I truly want.

Be You

I need you to be you,
and that is all I want.

I want you to become
the person you want to become.

Not for your friends
or family
or for the new promises
you make to yourself every year.

Become who you want
to become for the person
inside of you.

The one you let out
when no one is around.

That is the real you.

That is who you should be.

That is who I want to meet,
and that is who I want to love.

People think they know people, when really they do not. We were not meant to be understood. We are meant to go and all I see are the footprints you left behind.

The Last

The last conversation was always the worst.

This is something I have always thought.

But I ran into her a few years later.
And I discovered that the last conversation
isn't the worst.

It is the one you have the next time you
meet, accidentally of course.

"Why did you help find me if all you wanted
to do was leave me behind?
Why did you love me if in the end you left
all this pain behind?"

I had nothing to say . . .

"I don't hate you. I don't hate anyone
really."

Shocked at the questions she was asking.

She didn't even care to bother how I was
doing.

Women are like that at times.

They don't forget, so please watch out with
them.

"I just want to understand what it is like to
be an asshole, that is all," she said.

The words did not pour,
and that was unusual.

The words always pour.

Sometimes you are the asshole everyone
warns you about even
if you cannot see it for yourself.

Raindrops

You said I was the rain
for the way I fell
and I said you were a river
for the way you ran.

The way you ran from the pain
the whole goddamn world
had caused you.

And now, you are gone . . .
And now, all I have left
are the things I have
to make myself from:

from all the things
that are no longer here.

From the shatter in your eyes,
to what it is like to fall forever.

From all the things that used to matter,
to all the things that made me feel.

So keep running my friend, keep finding . . .

and I will do my best with falling
and finding as well.

What I Didn't Learn about You

And now
I set you free
among the wolves.

So please go,
go now,
go find them,
and kill them softly
with all the things
this earth has
never revealed to you.

Kill them all
with the love
you never had.

The Message I Wrote for Myself

And there was
nothing left to hurt . . .
That's how I knew
it was over.

And in the end,
I belonged to myself,
and I was finally able
to change—for me.

The love I had inside me
didn't belong to you
or anyone I ever knew . . .

It was all, ultimately,
meant for me.

I can not recognize my hands.
I do not know what they are made
for, if they are not touching
yours.

Say Something

I know you want to
say something.

I know you want to
save me, understand me,
but for some odd reason
the people that don't
know me, are the people
who really understand me.

They are the ones
who will help me save myself.

So yes, the world is
a terrible place.

You don't need to explain it any further.

I get it, believe me, I really do.

But sometimes it takes
a complete stranger
to help you realize
how you have the power
to get up, and put yourself
back together again.

Knowing All Is Knowing Nothing

They say I have to know you to love you.

You have to tell me things like
your favorite colors,
what kind of films you watch,
and what kind of music
you listen to, etc.

And then, possibly,
after knowing all those things about you,
I am supposed to see
if we are compatible with each other,
that is, if we have enough things
in common.

Well, I do not abide by those rules
and right now, I only want to know
what is in your mind,
all the things you are too afraid to say,
the rain you have within.

I want to know everything
that hurts and I only want to
love everything that is unreachable.

Deserve to Love

And I hope you find
more than just yourself.

I hope you find
the strength
not to hurt the people
who love you.

I hope you find
a thousand miracles
hidden in the soft rain.

And I hope you find art,
in all the people
you deserve to love.

Colors Change

I don't expect you
to be the same because
a lot has changed.

I mean, I'm not the same
person you remember me as.

I'm better, a lot better.

So to be real with you
I'm not interested
in the small talk, although
I do have a lot to get off my chest
on how careless you were
back then, but to be honest
I don't even care anymore
and that's the reality.

So let that sink for a while,
let that burn, let that eat the flesh,
because the truth is,
reality is reality
and sometimes reality knocks
the wind out of you.

I just don't really give a damn
to even witness it.

There are times when words cannot
explain how I feel and that is
okay, either way, thank you for
understanding my silence.

Miracles

And anything could happen here.

A miracle could happen.

You finding yourself
could happen.
Hell, maybe you
could even find someone
and fall in love . . .

Who knows . . .

All you have to do is believe.

Beautiful things happen
when you begin to believe.

Muse

I found almost everything
about her to be inspiring,
but I also found it
inspiring:

how we could
send a man to the moon,
how we could split atoms,
and how we could
communicate halfway
around the world . . .

But there was such a difference
in this new found inspiration.

It made me feel good
about myself and I found
that to be incredible.

She was like a dream,
and sometimes that's
what we all need.

A dream to help us
get through our daily lives.

We live in a bubble of fear, of
comfort and all we do is complain of
the things we do not have, of the
things we cannot touch and I cannot
break free without you. I need you.

A Little Fire

Keep a little fire going,
a little self-love,
and a little confidence.

Keep it hidden in you,
if you must,
but keep it—nonetheless.

Do not let it out
until you feel you must,
until it is the only thing
left to do.

And if it doesn't belong anywhere,
then create a place
where it would.

Let the whole world know
how your greatness started
from just one spark.

Show them why legends
never die.

She Part 3

She didn't know what she wanted
and she knew how no one ever did.

But she did know one thing:

She wanted to be found in the rain.

She wanted to run wild.

She wanted to fall, and feel safe,
but dangerous enough
to let her heart drop.

She wanted love,
true love, pure and kind and untouched.

The kind that wasn't ruined
by the chaos of the world.

The kind you would find
in a small coffee shop
in some foreign country.

That is all she really wanted,
and she didn't know where
or how it would appear,
but she knew, deep within her,

I rise like a flower from the
depths of my soul. I grow, I grow,
and all I do is wave at the people
as they come and go.

it would show itself
in the form of something
unexpected.

The Rocks inside You

There is something heavy
inside of you.

Something that is preventing
you from moving on.

I can see it in you.

I can see it in all of us.

We are all connected
by the same sorrow
and the same regret.

Eventually, without reason,
we learn from
their hidden truths.
We learn how a million
different things can go wrong,
and how a million
different things can go right.

Without pain and loss,
there is no perfect nirvana,
only such a place can
exist at the edge of
our doom.

Things I Once Saw

The people were too busy doing little things,
getting by.

You know, working the same ol' beat-up
jobs.

Driving the same ol' beat-up cars.

Dreaming the same ol' beat-up dream.

Waiting for something to free them from the
boredom.

And they wait and they wait.

As they live they wait to either
win the lottery or in some way
save the world.

They wait and then they wait some more . . .

But those who want to win the lottery don't
play enough
to win and those who want
to save the world don't believe
in themselves enough to save it.

They wait with their tired jobs, cars, and dreams.

You have got to take action, believe a little more, and maybe you might win the lottery.

You might even save the world.

Who knows, keep pushing, just know that there is something better on the other side.

Rise

Rise from the clear waters
of your soul and bloom
enough to drink the air
and wild of the sea.
Drown yourself
and be fueled by the fire
that breathes under the water.

Become the light.

Expose yourself to the light
for it lives in you,

and I promise

you will grow there.

I did not leave because of
you. I left because of me. I had
to go and yes, I do miss you
and I do love you but I love
myself more than anyone else,
and I deserve to work on myself
alone. Either way, I hope
you find what you are looking
for.

Tell Me the Truth

You should tell people
how you feel.

You should be open and truthful.

You should get up
every time you fall.

You should fight
for what is important.

By that I mean
all the things that keep you
up at night.

You should believe in every breath
that leaves your body.

You are a walking miracle.

You should laugh a little more.

It looks so fucking good on you.

You should do all these things,
but only when you are ready.

Everything will begin,
your world will begin,

but only when you are ready.

People Still Go

And I found myself asking why
certain people never came back.

And I asked myself why
I would always change
when someone would leave.

And I asked my mind,
several times,
why it would replay memories
that I had never lived.

And in the hour of silence,
I did discover one thing—
how everyone deserved
a chance to move on,
and how all was still
and only the people were moving.

Scared of It All

And you tell everyone
how much you have accomplished.

And you tell everyone
how much you are loved.

And you tell everyone
about all the adventures you have had.

And you tell everyone . . .

and tell everyone . . .

and tell everyone everything
about you.

And still,
in the middle of the crowd,
you feel more alone than ever.

You wonder why
eventually they all leave.

Sometimes people are only interested
in things you are too afraid to say.

STOP! You have less than five seconds
to think of someone, pick up your
phone and tell them you love them.
Do it now, every second is a mystery.

The String of Your Soul

And every day . . .
let something pull you in.

And every day . . .
let something catch your attention.

And every day . . .
find something new.

And everyday . . .
find summer in all winters.

And every day . . .
fly toward the sun.

And everyday . . .
feel beautiful (because you are).

And everyday . . .
discover how love does not fade.

And everyday . . .
find growth: quietly.

Live this way and everyday you will
be closer to the perfect version of you.

Everyday is important, if only
you gave it and yourself a chance.

Sadness is an ocean and sometimes
I drown while other times I have
no choice but to swim.

And Now

And now they have departments
for everything you own.

For your car,
for your house,
for your kids,
for your money,
for your school,
and even your own dreams.

And they can, if they wanted to,
take it all away.

Not even the people you love belong to you.

Death is always waiting in the back of the
show . . . that, and they want you to think it
all belongs to you.

And what a shame it is how nothing is ever
really yours . . .

The only thing you own is your debt
and you carry it with you as if it is pushed
by your skin.

Debt is inevitable . . .

Nothing more.
Nothing less.

The Truth

The truth is never easy
but it should come out of you
like breath, like the life
you hold within.

Speak of it
and one day the love
lost in your eyes
will take you to
another place.

The one that is waiting for you
to be revealed.

In The Middle of the Street

There are some people
who come into your life
with a light so bright
they make you forget
where you are.

Find these people
and live in their suns.

You are their planets

and you are their moons.

And that is how life is meant to be lived.

How people are meant to be loved.

Be someone's light,
even in the middle of the street.

I break things, that is the only
thing I know how to do, and
sometimes you break me and because
of it, I love you.

Something New

And then there are the people
who will buy something new,
go somewhere different,
and even switch crowds
to feel better about themselves.

But what they fail to understand is,
true happiness
doesn't work this way.

You have to find it from within.

So no matter where you go,
what you buy, or who you
spend your time with . . .

your demons will still be with you,
and you have to find a way
to bury them
before they go ahead
and bury you instead.

Do Not Be Like Them

Do not be like them.

Do not be like one of those
sad people who complain
about sad things.

They go on to live sad lives.

Be not like them.

Be different.

Be you.

Be happy.

And you will find the light in you without
even realizing it . . .

That I promise.

They Say

"They say when someone leaves, something
inside of you dies, but
they also say something inside of you is
born."

That must have been the line that set me off,
that set off this whole writing gig.

My friend of twenty-plus years called me
over the telephone.

Now, I hate phone calls,
I hate text messages,
and most of the time,
I hate communication, period.

(Ironic enough?)

It had been a long time since we spoke.

She was one of those friends, the kind who
disappear on you as soon as they enter a
relationship.

I guess she had been going through some
tough waters because that's the only time
she would call me.

We did the casual talk and then we talked
about what she called me for, obviously.

"I don't understand how you can spend so
much time with someone,
and then in an instant, they are gone," she
said.

"That's life. People come and go."

"I just don't feel the same anymore,
and now I feel more trapped within myself,
more than ever, more than before," her voice
trembled as if it was her last word.

"Because some people can do that to you,
kid. Some people can free you from
yourself," I said.

Soon after we hung up and I replayed those
two sentences over and over . . .

"They say when someone leaves, something
inside of you dies, but they also say
something inside of you is born."

Like a windmill caught in a hurricane,
those words kept cycling and cycling all
over my head, over and over with no bounds
of no end . . .

And I am still trapped within myself, but I
still think

those were the wisest words I have ever
heard.

Those sparks you see coming out
of me are my thoughts and feelings
and sometimes they are all about
you.

Rebel Again

If you must rebel,
then rebel for a cause.

Do not riot into the night
for nothing.

If you must,
do it for change.

Do it for people.

Do it for all the things
that might kill you.

But above all,
do it for life.

It is all worth more
when you do it for life.

I Forgive You, My Love

And I forgive you for everything
you did not do.

It was not your fault.

You did not know how to be good,
how to love.

You did not know anything
about people or the way they
carried themselves
when they were hurt.

I forgive you.

I forgive you for leaving
when I needed you the most.

And now, in the aftermath,
I cannot even understand
my own language.

I do not know where I am
and I do not know who I have become.

And I just want to find myself
where I least expect it . . .

in the middle of my smile,
where my inspiration dwells.

No One Cares

But no one cares
and when they do
they want to make it seem
like it is all about you.

But their agenda is different
and it is always different.

It can be about money,
about fame,
about getting ahead,
but the similarity is
it doesn't concern you.

And you might think,
maybe they do care about me.

Maybe they do want to help me.

But in the end, it is mostly
all the same.

People want to use you.

So I feel you, Mr. Dylan,
when you say the times they are a-changin'.

Yes, they are changing and no
one gives a damn about anything
other than themselves.

Last Choice

If it is not you
then I want no one,
in this life and in the next.

You would be my first
and my last choice.

I love you
and I want you like a man
who has nothing:

in little daydreams,
in light whispers,
every day,
all the time.

Believe in people and you will
grow in all the places they never
thought you would.

Becoming

And then
you became that place
I couldn't visit anymore.

That song
I couldn't listen to.

That memory
I couldn't relive.

That one night
I couldn't go back to.

You became everything
I wish I had.

Changing Matters

And now it is all different.

It has all changed
and she was more,
and there was more to her
than her fire.

Wild in love in all her
drunken glory . . .

She was everything I wanted.

She the ocean,
the sunset,
and all the best parts I fell into.

She was everything that
had ever made me feel
a little more.

She Has Too Much

"The girl has too much attitude.
Stay away from her," they say.

"She's trouble. Hard to love, hard to
understand, hard to control and run with."

Hell, they can make any woman look like a
nightmare but those bastards
have it all wrong.

Women like that, the ones with too much
fire inside, need something else and it is not
something you can find in stores.

They need a little bit more than that.

A little more soul,
a little more truth,
and above all, a little more love.

Strange things happen when I am
alone. I think of you and I fall.
I think of you and I ache. I think
of you and I fly. Most days, I feel
alone and sometimes I feel invincible.

Broken Lightbulbs

I want to live in a place
where love isn't a metaphor for sex
and silence isn't a metaphor for fear.

Where if you are laughing all day,
you're not considered crazy,
and if you want to actually help someone,
it's not to expect something in return.

Where small talk doesn't exist
and people genuinely care.

And where you
and I are closer together.

Imagine what a beautiful thing it can be.

I want to go there.

I want to grow old there and above all,
I want to love there.

Scarecrows and Clouds

Life is frightening.

Of course, anyone can tell you that,
but more frightening than life itself is not
knowing how it would turn out.

Like the you from five years ago would tell
the you of today,

"Well, that's odd. I didn't expect that to
happen."

And that's okay,
because nothing goes the way you picture it.

Nothing is ever really planned.

Life is full of surprises,
even when you expect something to happen.

Don't Ask Me

Don't ask me to leave because I might stay.

Don't ask me to stay because I might leave.

No one ever wants to be told how to live.

People don't work that way,
never have and never will.

So if I say I want you,
it doesn't mean I expect you to want me
back. That's not how it works.

If you want something you have to earn it.

You have to risk everything
for all the things you want to keep.

I Am a Diamond

You didn't destroy me.

I'm still here.

I'm still laughing and dancing
and getting myself back together.

You see, you didn't break me.

I broke myself
and most people have this terrible
misunderstanding of what hurts.

You see, if I loved you,
that's because I fell into it,
not because you pushed me off the edge.

I jumped.

I fell.

I got hurt.

Me. Me. Me.

And right now it's all about me.

So I'm sorry you came all this way to
apologize.

I don't need that,
and I'm sorry you came all this way for
nothing.

We go to places to to seek
adventure, to find ourselves.
well, I say, I go to places
to find things that remind me
of you.

Make You Sad

I do not want to make you sad
or make you cry.

No, never that.

I want to make you remember,
make you realize.

I want you to take in life,
all of it, completely.

I want you to acknowledge terrible things
and beautiful things
and how not all good is good
and not all bad is bad.

That's all I want.

I want you to believe in yourself
and not panic if something goes wrong,
because some hearts do get broken
and some hearts never fully heal and
sometimes there are no happy endings, and
that's okay.

You'll get through it.

You're strong enough.

I know it.

The Girl in the Bookstore

It's as if she contradicts herself.

She wants it all
but she doesn't know what to do with it.

She wants the day
but she is far too in love with the night.

She wants to understand herself
but she doesn't know where to begin.

And then I thought . . .
how everyone was like this.

No one really knew what they wanted
and when they did they want more.

We are all the same person after all.

Sunset

And there she goes,
walking as if she's dragging
the sun beneath her feet.

She goes, as she splits the atoms:

the ones of men and the ones of gods.

She doesn't break.

She consumes and then planets are born.

She is all things that are not here,
everything we see
but everything we could never
understand.

Allow yourself to be picked.
Allow yourself to break.
Allow yourself to hurt.
Open yourself to all these things
and you will appreciate everything
most people tend to ignore.

Everything Is Every Thing

Every door leads somewhere.

Every chance is a blessing.

Every song, every movie,
and every book is another world.

Every person you meet will
change your direction.

Every person you love will
strengthen your connection.

(The one to yourself.)

Every moment you spend looking,
something breathtaking will be
found. And above all,
every time you feel broken,
someone will be there
to help you heal.

You have to hope for all of these
and believe in them . . .
so you can learn to live better.

This is how you will find paradise.

All Broken Flowers Grow

I want to see you grow.

I want to see you for who you are.

I want ten years to pass,
so you could come back
and tell me how much you've loved,
how much you've learned.

I want to see you inspired
and touched by the flames inside you.

I want to see you do all the things we both
know you're capable of . . .

But I can't help you
if you can't help yourself,
because I believe in all the things that
move inside you.

So give yourself a chance
and I will be here
just in case you ever fall.

Boundaries

"I'm tired of living with boundaries.
I need to know what these wings can do. I
need to find out. Maybe my calling is out
there," she said, as they sat on the edge of
the building watching the city from above.

"No, sweet little love.

Your genius.

Your beauty.

Your struggle.

Your art.

Everything you'll ever need isn't out there.
Everything is in you.

Believe in yourself.

Fall within yourself.

That's where you'll fly.

That's where you'll expand your wings."

The Return

And sometimes
the one who left you broken returns.

And sometimes
they are different and sometimes
they show you how much they've changed.

And that alone might be one of the greatest
things in the world . . .

to have someone you once cared about
go through the trouble of finding you,
just to tell you
how much they still care.

Come away with me and I promise
you, you will never feel the
burn of pain ever again.

Falling

You fall and break
because you are soft and fragile.

You fall and break
because you have too much inside you,
too much love and too much feeling,
and it is enough to cure the hatred in the
world.

You fall and break
for the people you care about
and sometimes the ones you barely even
know.

You fall and break
because sometimes you just have to
and because sometimes it is the right thing
to do.

So keep falling and keep breaking,
little bird.

It is, after all,
what makes you beautiful.

It is, after all, what makes you who you are.

And to be honest, I have never been more attracted to anyone in my life.

I think I need you and I think you need me.

The Last Sentence

This is the last thing I want to tell you.

I want you to put yourself first,
no matter who you fall in love with.

I want you to love yourself
like it's the only thing left to do.

And lastly,
I want you to find someone
that will help you realize how important the
first two things are.

Your life should consist of making yourself
happy before giving your laughter away to
someone else.

Just Because

Because deep down inside you,
the sun rises and the moon sets.

Because deep down inside you,
there's more than what most people see:

an ocean deep enough to drown the world.

Because deep down inside you,
there's a love
and it's connected to the way the planets
move.

Because deep down inside you,
there's fire and snow,
life and death, strength and weakness,
and they're all fighting for your attention.

Because deep down inside you,
such places do exist and all places need to
be found, and they're all in you,

all you have to do . . .
is believe.

Memory is a funny little thing.
It can give you all the pleasure
in the world or it can give you
all the ache it has to offer.
There is no in-between, that is
life and sometimes that is love.

Birds

"She became everything that was around me. She became these places, ones I knew existed but I had never gone to. She became everything I wasn't and everything I was."

"Then why did you let her go?"

"I didn't let her go. I set her free. She's like a bird, and all wild birds should be free."

"Keeping her caged would have killed her."

Complicated Things

I am only interested in complicated things.
So do not give me what is easy,
that I do not want.

Give me the things you do not understand.

Give me the oceans you are too afraid to
swim in, and the trees you cannot climb
because they scare you.

Give me all the parts of you that you are
afraid of.

Give me what worries you,
what tears you apart.

If you are broken, then I will mend you.

I will dance with your fears
and make love to everything that makes you
feel alone.

Face the World

You should go out
and face the world as you once did
when you were young.

See the sky in different shades
and the trees for more than what they are.

You should stand beneath the rain
and feel more than little droplets of water
rushing through your skin.

You should wrap everything with your
imagination, by that I mean people and
places, and find the inspiration to make
things better.

This is how we will survive.
This is how we will wander away,
but ultimately find each other again.

I Used to Love You

And I loved you
for the way you wrote
music on my skin.

And you loved me
for the way I played
the strings on your hair
and together we made love
in such a way
that artists do
when they create their works
of art.

But in the end,
none of that mattered,
for you were just another music lover,
and I
was just another one
of your songs.

One Day

One day,
you will realize
how there are some people
who are not meant
to be yours.

One day,
you will have to
move on,
and sometimes
the most important thing
to do
is to let go.

We come and we go but none of us
have the courage to stay.

Think Too Much

You think too much
of all the things you want,
so you have forgotten
what it is you need.

And you don't need much, kid.

You just need a few good people,
and very few will carry love in their hearts.

So please,
stop over thinking.

Stop chasing the wrong things.

Listen to your friends.

Listen to the ones who love you
and understand how things change
but the love they have for you
will always remain.

Drunk One Night Prose

Everyone needs
someone to hold on to,
and I'm glad you exist,
for without you
I could never imagine
what this world
would be like.

Thank you.

Thank you.

Thank you.

Without you,

I am nothing.

Matters of the Heart

One of the hardest things
to do in the world is . . .

to convince our minds
the doings of our hearts,
and trying to explain
to one another
why the other exists.

Another Night Drunk Prose

To all the artists
that have influenced me,
I love you.

Although we will probably never meet.

I just want you to know
how your music,
your poetry,
and your art
has saved my life.

And how it has made me
feel less alone.

Thank you for all that you do.

Thank you for saving me.

And thank you for making my life
a little more than what it is.

Eventually it all hurts and yes,
I know things do get better but
the days between now and then
are the hardest to come by. I
just hope I could survive another
storm until the sun comes back
into my life.

It Is Always Okay

It's okay to feel alone,
lost and empty.

For everything that's lonely
finds its company.

Everything lost is meant to be found
and everything empty eventually gets filled.
So see it like this:

Think about all the terrible times you have
lived through, and think about how they,
too, have passed.

You're a survivor
and you have to go through hell to find
heaven.

The same way you must break in order to
find yourself whole again.

Legend

But greatness is usually frowned upon
and ignored.

But the secret is to keep building.

No one is going to pay attention at first,
but if you keep going,
eventually someone will notice.

But you should never do it
for other people.

Do it for yourself.

Build it for yourself
and your future.

No one ever cares about the brick,
but everyone will stop
and marvel at the giant wall.

Feel Too Much Part 2

It hurts because you feel too much,
because you care too much,
and because you feel connected
no matter how far you go.

So to be honest,
it will always hurt,
and you will go through life thinking
it is such a terrible thing.

But, my dear,
it is not,
and I want you to keep feeling,
keep caring,
and keep loving,
for all those things do bring pain.

But I assure you,
it is all quite worth it.

In other words,
I need you to be you
when I need you most.

Be Gentle

Be gentle and kind.

Be fragile and soft.

I know the world tells you otherwise,
but deep down inside
you are not what they want you to be.

You are all things that change . . .
all leaves that fall,
all rain that meets the ground,
and all petals that the flower
can no longer hold.

So if you are meant to shatter,
then go ahead, break beautifully,
for the more you fall,
the more you rise and the more you do both,
the easier it will be to
find yourself again.

Believe me, I know how you feel
and I know what it is like to have
the whole damn world against you,
watching you, hoping one day you
would fall, but you cannot fall
you are stronger than that. I
believe it and so should you.

Things Happen

Things happen.

No one likes sudden movement.

No one wants to be pushed off the edge
while they're not ready to fly.

People get stirred.

People get forced into certain situations
and when they do, they change.

No matter how far they run, they change!

You'll change.

I'll change
and sooner or later we'll be different.

The world will be different
but the love we have for each other
will always be the same.

Sadness

And it is sad how people come and go.

It is almost too beautiful to bear,
the way people gently come into our lives
to leave just as softly.

But that's life, right?

We make memories with other people
to remember them once they're gone.

We exchange experiences and expect to
learn something valuable in-between.

The same way we have to learn to let go
and the same way we have to learn
how to embrace change as it comes.

And that's what makes this life beautiful,
for it is the coming and the going that makes
us who we are.

Feeling Lost Prose

We hurt ourselves
by loving other people
and I think we're all okay
with a little pain.

Feeling Lost Prose Part 2

The right person
can make you remember
or forget—all the moments
that took your breath away.

The view from up here is beautiful.
I could see it all, from the
look in your eyes to the way
your mouth moves. I want to kiss
you. I never want to come back
down again.

Don't Sink

You don't have to sink to the bottom of the
ocean and watch the world as you fall.

You don't have to isolate yourself
because you're hurt.

People who love you will always be waiting
near the shore and every once in a while
it's okay to come to the surface to breathe.

We all need air to grow.

We all need an ocean to let go,
but it's people who will save you.

Always remember that.

Manufacturing Love

The things I want
cannot be bought or made in large
quantities.

The things I want
are simple and do not worry the heart.
The things I want
can only be given once in a lifetime
and at any given moment.

And it is not love,
no it is not that!

I want laughter, freedom, and self-
expression.

I want all the art that defines me.

All the things that hit me hard enough to
move me in such ways
the world has never seen.

This Woman

And that was the problem.

I wanted to get away.

I wanted to be as far away as possible.

That was the only way I could have
understood you and I didn't want to leave
but I did it anyway.

And to be honest,
I did it to feel closer to you.

So I could come back to give you
the love you deserved.

What She Said to Me One Night

I have too much
universe in me.
I deserve more
than the sky
and a few stars.

People Are Liars

People are liars.

They say strong hearts do not break,
wild hearts can be controlled,
and heavy hearts remain on the ground.

Well, this I say to you.

The strongest hearts do shatter,
the wildest hearts do roam free,
and the heaviest hearts do fly
and never come down.

So next time, please don't listen to other
people.

So many are full of shit.

Break if you must,
find freedom because you need it to grow,
and fly beyond the imagination.

You must find yourself, love yourself,
before finding others like you who
understand.

No More Love Please

You say you will not love again,
how your last relationship really
destroyed you
and how love doesn't exist anymore.

Well, I say you're a liar,
for you will learn to love again
and every time you do,
it will hurt a little more than the last.

I just hope you find it
when you least expect it.

The best kind of lovers
are the ones who arrive
without a proper invitation.

I keep coming back to the ocean
and I think it is because you felt
free there. I am your breeze and
you are my ocean and together we
will always be dreams to those who
are willing to look.

Breaking Atoms

We break because we are fragile.

We cry because what's inside
is too much to bear.

We hurt because the pain
doesn't know where else to go
and we feel
because other people feel
and that's how we know we're connected.

And we search through life looking
for others like us, for the ones who
break, cry, and hurt.

And we feel them, we love them,
and grow with them, and together,
if we believe enough,
we will inspire the world
and learn how to make it beautiful again.

Sooner or Later

Sooner or later
you are going to find that place
you have been looking for
and it will pour there
and you will run beneath the rain
and stretch your arms there.

You will welcome the storm
and you will feel all the things
that stir inside you.

You will be happy there.

You will be free and you will find the
inspiration to love again.

Start to End

The same way it begins,
it ends,
and when it is over,
you realize how loving someone
and forgetting them is the same.

You realize
how night can sometimes be day
and how laughter can sometimes be tears.

You realize
so many things when someone is gone.

You realize
who you are and how much love you have
given
to those who do not deserve it.

And to be honest,
in the end,
there is nothing worse to realize,
other than that.

Time Heals

Give yourself the time to heal.

It is okay to get your heart broken.

It is okay to shatter
and slip through the cracks a few times.

For the world wants you to believe
that loving yourself is an illness
but none of that is true.

Take the time to love yourself.

Your body isn't broken.

Your body is marvelous
and you are more than what
they expect you to be.

You are everything they could never
understand: love and light mixed together
and all things that blow with the wind.

Openness

I don't know much about this world
but I do know one thing.

When people open their hearts
they find the courage to do remarkable
things.

So keep your heart open.

I wouldn't worry about anything else.

Find Her

And she did find her pieces in other people,
because ultimately,
that's what she would look for.

She found her smile
in a small boy in San Francisco.

She found her laughter
watching a couple in the middle of Chicago.
She found her dreams
listening to music one night in New York
City.

And she never stopped finding new things
about herself.

She went on and became more.

She became whole
and she was happy
and for the rest of her life
she found the inspiration she needed
to become the type of woman she had

always

dreamed of.

Walk Away

And we should be together.

And my mind can't agree
with my heart. And my heart
is filled with endings, ones
without beginnings. And it
stings when I think about it.

And the slightest thought
sets me off. And I feel sad
but this is not a sad letter.

And my heart is an instrument,
a symphony of feelings
too beautiful to bear.

What I'm trying to say is,
I can't remember anything else,
other than the moment
you walked away.

You are the only person I think of
when I am alone near the shore, and
I wish you could be here. I have
so much I want to share with you.

Connected to You

I want to feel connected to you.

I want a string to be tied
from your heart to mine,
so we don't lose each other in the transition.

I've lost too many people,
too many feelings,
and too many things that have taken
my breath away.

I've been that person,
the one who's been taken for granted
one too many times
and I've suffered enough because of it.

I just want to know if this is real,
if we're real,
and if everything around us
brings us closer together.

That's all I want
and I think everyone wants that.

I think everyone needs someone
to remind them
how to fall in love with themselves.

Midnight Prose Again

Maybe something good
will come out of this
and it will be something
I was meant for...

like tasting the stars
on your lips
and watching the flowers
bloom out of your skin.

I'm ready

and

I love you.

Live

When things break
they never feel the same
and that's what made
whatever it was we had—sad.

We lasted
but not long enough.

We were close but not close enough.
And when it was over,
it was hard to be anything else,
when you were nothing more than just
another experience
and I was just another person
who lived through it all.

Strange Expression

And I found it strange
how the people who were in love
couldn't express their love
and the people who were hurt
were always hurt.

And then,
they would trade positions,
like an off-and-on switch
and avoided one another at all costs.

And it was even stranger how
I, too, was like this.
I was lost between love and pain
and at any given moment
I would stumble and fall in love
to get up and fall in pain.

And this happened all of the time.

I was a walking contradiction
and as time went on
I never knew where I was going to end up.

I never knew who I was going to become.

Something to Remember

Because I know
in the bottom of your heart
there's a crack
and that's how the warmth gets in.
And because of that,
you shouldn't worry.

Always remember,
no matter how dark it gets,
the light will always be
on your side.

It Was Never for You

And sometimes
you realize how some people
are too damn heavy.

How sometimes letting go
is the only option
and how sometimes
the only way we can learn to fly
is if we stop chasing
the people
who were never meant for us
at all.

Keep Going

There will always be
battles between the mind and the heart.

Between
the things you know
and the things you feel.

Between
what you want and what you need.

Between
who you are and who you want to be.

So remember,
tomorrow is a new day
and you will always have a chance to
succeed.

Keep going and stay strong.

You Have It in You

Miracles are happening
inside you
and everyday they are waiting
on the edge of the earth
to change people's lives.

All you have to do
is give yourself a chance.

You have all the fires
and all the winds
to make this world a better place.

Fix You

The person who broke your heart
will not fix you,
the person who left you
will not come back to save you,
and the person who put you down
will not lift you into the air.

Now what you make of all three is up to
you,
but it is always recommended
to ask them to go fuck off,
politely and kindly if necessary.

Time moves strangely when you are in love and sometimes when I am with you, I forget where I am.

Back Together to Fall Apart

You will never stop putting yourself back
together.

You will never stop breaking
and you will never stop pouring yourself
into all the things you love.

You will never stop, never,
because you are gentle, beautiful,
and delicate.

Because all human life is fragile
and all human life should be handled with
care.

So slowly shatter into the earth,
softly pour yourself into the ocean,
and quietly pile yourself back together
again.

Doing so is what makes the light in you
something worth stopping for
and every time I do,
you take my breath away.

And I appreciate that.

Drink to the Art

Because sometimes that movie,
that song,
and that painting say more about you
than you can about yourself.

Because sometimes that book
has your story and because sometimes
you have to believe in others.

That's the power of art.

We use it to communicate with others.

We use it to feel less alone.

ROBERT M. DRAKE

She Left

And when she's gone . . .

I hope people remember her
for all the little things she left
behind.

For the art she
made while she was being
herself and for the way she
inspired people to love
all over again.

Too Beautiful for Words

You should let others see the goodness in
you.

It's too damn beautiful to ignore.

You should let it out.

Let it pour.

I know it's hard to be judged.

I know hateful people,
people who have not yet found themselves,
make it hard for others to live,
and I know sad people don't stay sad
forever.

So listen to yourself . . .

love yourself a little more.

You deserve to.

Don't waste your time in things that empty
you. Save yourself.

Only you can do that.

Pay Attention

And if you pay
close attention,

you will find
the gentle poetry
in all places:

between all the things
that make me miss you
and all the things
that make me fall for you,
all over again.

We are here. This is our generation and we are beat up and tired. We no longer believe in your rules and we came here to change your old ways. Do not fuck with us. We are not playing. We are here to take all the things that do not belong to you.

Changing Directions

And there were times
when she felt lost.

But that did not stop her,
for the farther she went,
The more she collected herself
as she walked away
and the more she walked away
the closer she got to it all.

In the end,
she became more than what she expected.
She became the journey,
and like all journeys,
she did not end.

She just simply changed directions
and kept going.

The Time Walks with You

But it is the smallest things
you miss when you lose someone.

Like the last kiss you shared
and the last time you looked into their eyes.

Those are the things that kill you.

Those are the things you take with you
as time goes by.

Lose It All

We all have to lose
our minds a little.

We all have to follow
our hearts blindly
and we all have to walk
through the fire
no matter how bad it gets.

That is how you will find
the things you need
to believe again.

That is how you
will find your way
back home.

What Friends Do

It's okay
to collapse into
my arms.

You don't always
have to be strong.

You don't always
have to fight.

I am here,
and believe me
when I tell you,
I have your back

and

I will protect you
till the very end.

Beautiful Girl

Beautiful girl,
the peace you've been searching for
can be found in your heart.

So let it ache, let it fall,
for underneath those untamed forces
you will find your love.

Your ultimate silence,
a truth the world will always be
too afraid to hear.

Broken Wings

But leaving is an art,
and I have painted enough
birds with broken wings . . .

And I have watched them go
into the horizon,
for they have learned
how to fly again
and I have learned how to
let them go.

ROBERT M. DRAKE

Some times I do not have much to say, and I know I should tell you the way you make me feel but I will not. I rather show you. I rather prove my love than cover your heart with a collection of empty words.

322

Beautiful Chaos

She's so beautiful,
you could almost feel the sun breaking
around her
as she walks into a daydream . . .

like a runaway child
and she exhales devastation
like the last time you said her name.

Small Fires Start Bigger Fires

She loves out of mind,
out of what hurts . . .

and that's why she wants to save you,
because deep down she's the type of woman
who wants to fix broken things . . .

So to be with her
you must understand,
how her heart is strong enough to heal the
world.

Home Again

I woke up feeling everything again.

I woke up remembering
how it all began and how it all ended . . .

and I thought
how maybe love was a lot like this.

How maybe
one day I would be able to wake up
in your heart
and learn to call it home again.

The Reveal

There is life in the moment
right before a kiss,
and some will argue it is poetry
but I believe it is more.

I believe it is our hearts revealing secrets
our lips could never reveal to each other
or to ourselves.

She Is Stars and Moons

And if there's a universe in her,
then by all means let it be free,
let it be born,
and let it carry this pain
within me out of my body.

Let it be worth more than a
thousand lovers
and a million I love yous.

Let her stars and moons
be my church and let
loving her be my only religion.

1999 Prose

And as you walked away,
I sat back and laughed
at the love
I was never meant to have.

I present you a flower. It is filled
with my deepest memories. I want you
to have it. So please do not lose it,
if you do you will lose me forever.
Keep me and remember me whenever you
are sad.

Make Me Feel

They say a picture
is worth a thousand words

and I can't seem to wonder

how you see
a thousand different things

but none of them define
how you feel.

She Came Looking

And at times,
she didn't know many things.

She didn't know
if she wanted to remain lost
or if she wanted someone
to come looking for her.

She didn't know if she wanted to stay
or if she wanted to go.

She didn't know who she was
or who she was meant to be . . .

but she did know one thing.

She knew she wanted someone
to fall in love with her heartbeat
before they fell in love
with anything else she had to offer.

Kiss Kiss

And tonight we are together
and tonight is far more
perfect than the night before.

And tonight we whisper
and tonight it is all about you.

And tonight I think I love you more
and tonight the sky is full
of old literature.

And tonight they all say the same thing.

"Kiss her well and make her
forget who she is."

The Cycle

And we can't let go
because we hold on
like it's never going to happen again,
but it does and it will.

It all repeats itself over
and over again.

Universe

Sometimes it's okay to be alone.

It's okay not to know or even care.

You don't always need someone.

You don't always need to know where
you're going, for you have loved
and cared far enough.

This time,
you should think about yourself . . .

love yourself,
be alone with yourself,
and do everything you need to do for
yourself. Believe . . .

and you will find the edge of the universe
within you.

Running Away

And all your life
you thought
breaking free
meant you were fighting
to move forward,
but in reality,
you were only walking
farther away.

We are not meant to be held
forever, therefore, you should
catch me now before someone else
does.

I Wasn't Inspired

And as time passed
she felt better about herself
and her life.
She let herself go,
the same way lovers let go.

She knew things were about
to change for the best.

And like all things
that were worth it,
she took a chance,
and she did it without regret,
without hurt,
and without her guard up.

The Stars Are Not Too Far

And you will remain far yet near.

Like the wind rushing through our hair.

Like the reason distant stars
only appear in the dark.

And like all
things that come close
but not enough to make our own.

I Am with You

I don't know many things.

Like why people leave
and why things happen the way they do . . .

but I do know one thing.

I know how I feel when you say
I am yours
and I know who I am
when I am with you
and I wouldn't change a thing
about that.

Wine and Poems

Because there is nothing in her
I would change,
for she is made of wine
and unfinished poems,
and her past tastes a lot like sadness
and winter rain.

And I love her at her best
and even harder at her worst.

She takes me to a reality
that has never existed,
and sometimes,
I am lost beneath her ribcage
without looking for a way out.

Open Your Eyes

All the lies you tell yourself
to get through the day,
then a new day arrives
and this is how you continue
to live your life . . .

and somehow
you're okay with this.

You're okay with pretending
to be other people
rather than yourself.

I have seen the world and I cannot
seem to wonder how none of those
places matter because you are not
here.

I Need You

And perhaps,
one day,
we will learn the difference
between the want
and the need
of another person.

Perhaps,
one day,
you will walk back
into my life
because you need to
and not
because I want you
to stay.

Myself and Me

I'm good at breaking my own heart.

I'm good at piecing myself back together
and there's nothing you could do to destroy
me.

So if it hurts . . .

it's only because I did this to myself
and I wouldn't have it any other way.

The Hardest Thing to Do

And as she walked away,
I finally understood
how sometimes the hardest thing to do
is to let another person
love you.

Prayers about You

But my heartaches grow
from all the places you have
touched
and now I am left with a garden
full of prayers
and they are all about you.

Maybe Who Knows

Maybe one day
we'll finally learn to love ourselves
and stop apologizing
for the things that make us
who we are.

I drop my eyes on the sky and let the wind carry me home. I let my sadness become my wall and I protect my love with my solitude. You have to feel what I feel to understand me and once you do, you realize I am just like you.

When She Was Young

Her ribcage
isn't built to harbor
so much pain,
and yet
she walks into an ocean
of darkness
and finds the inspiration
to burst
into a billion stars.

Chaos

Somewhere within her,
maybe
in the marrow of her bones . . .
there are a thousand cities.

And yet
she speaks of chaos
as if she doesn't know
what lies beneath
her chest.

I Love You More

I know you're broken
and I don't say this
just to say it,
but I know you've been
through hell and back
and it has changed you.

You're not the same person
I once knew
and it's not that I want
to fix you
or save you
or anything that has to do
with that.

It's more like
I will accept you
and take your flaws
for more than what they are.

If you're a hurricane
then I'll be the sea
that gives you the strength
to go on.

Writing on the Earth

I am not too afraid
to fall into the ocean

but every time I do
I think
how there would never be
enough sand for me
to write about all the things
you make me feel.

Save Yourself

You don't need
someone to save you.

Maybe what you need
is someone to teach you
how you are worth saving
and show you
how that is something
only you can do
for yourself.

Dear friend, as you fall and as you break, I cannot help but to collect your pieces. You are beautiful and I will make you whole again.

Roots from Broken Flowers

You can get yourself
into certain situations
but I can assure you,
every time you overcome something
you won't be the same person . . .

and it's the same idea
with every person you meet.

You cross paths,
exchange memories,
and from there on
you're someone else,
and how you grow from it
is entirely up to you.

The Things I Can't Tell Myself

I broke my own heart chasing you,
saving you, and loving you.

And I lost a lot of time doing so,
but this time
it's all about me.

So you can't come back demanding my
attention.

That's not how this works.

You can't just make an entrance
when the door
has been closed for so long.

People Like Us

You can't stop
certain things from happening.

You have to stop trying to control
everything.

Sometimes
you're going to lose.

Sometimes
you're going to be last.

The world wasn't built on perfection.

It was built day by day
and by people like us.

Fly Fly Fly

"I feel free with you," she said.

"Why?" he replied.

His eyes scanned through the room as if he were reading her feelings on the wall.

"Because you inspire me and that alone might be the most dangerous gift a person can present to another. You give me the courage I need to get my inner spirit going, and because of that I now believe how you don't need a pair of wings to fly."

I will meet you on the other
side, just promise me that you
will return back home.

I Appreciate You

I know you feel as if you're not appreciated.

I know you've let so many people in,
thinking maybe this time it will work out,
maybe this time
I have found the one I'm supposed to live
for.

I know every time someone leaves,
you lose a little more of your humanity,
you lose your hope.

I know all these things about you,
not because your eyes
have this tamed sadness within them,
but because I, too,
understand what it's like to love
and be unloved at the same time . . .

And I, too,
understand what it's like
to have a heart made of firewood.

I burn for the things I desire,
and like you,
all I really want is for someone
to fill my heart with adventure.

Sea, Sand, and Skies

We are the same,
you and I.

We fall in love
with the stars that don't belong to us
instead of the ones
burning in our hands.

We fall in love
with the breaking instead of the healing.

We fall in love
with drowning instead of the sea.

And we fall in love
with our memories instead of our future.

Read This Every Day

How many people
do you have to fall in love with
until you finally understand
that only person
you owe yourself to . . .
is you.

Afraid of What Is There

It's okay not to know
how to handle your own heart.

You should be afraid of it.

It roars,
it shifts,
it changes direction . . .

It does all these powerful things
and still,
it fits in one hand
and shatters the moment
the one you love let's it
slip away.

Too Hard to Understand

You lost her
and it wasn't because
she was hard to hold,
or love,
or touch,
but because she was made
of your absence,
of all the things you ignored
and all the beautiful poetry
you read but failed to understand.

I am not sure what to feel about
anything anymore. I am not even
sure who I am, but when I am with
you, everything makes sense and
I feel more like myself than I
have ever been.

Terrible Lives

Because some people
live these terribly confused lives.

They have it all backward.

They think love
is the fear of abandonment.

They think love is attachment
and what is worse is,
they think love is forcing someone
to stay.

Bloom

You don't need
someone's attention
to feel important.

You bloom off the top
of your eyes.

Open them.

See the possibility.

The world is far more inspiring
when you see it
for the first time.

For So Long

And one day,
you will understand
how some people feel familiar
the moment you meet them . . .

as if your souls have met many years ago
and they pick up
right where they left off.

And one day,
out of the blue,
someone will run up to you
and tell you . . .

"I have been waiting for you
and I have missed you for so long."

Anyone Else Is Not for Me

I know there are other people
out there I could possibly
fall in love with
and I know
how I might have a better shot
of happiness
but what's the point?

I found you
and you speak to me in ways
I can't imagine,
and because of that
I don't care about anyone else
other than you.

Sad Eyes

I know you're hiding something
behind those sad eyes.

You're afraid to show your soul
but I'm telling you to trust me.

Trust me with every atom that holds you
together.

I want to know the real you,
the you that knows silence,
abandonment, and pain.

The you the world isn't ready for.

Life is hard as it is,
for there is no reason to make loving you
even harder.

If you move too fast you will
miss the point. You will miss
the little things and I need you
to remember me before I go.

Sometimes

I can't apologize
for who I am,
but I can apologize
for the things I do
and I can't love you
without hurting you.

The same way
I can't hold on to your heart
without letting it slip
through my hands.

Sometimes I break
the things I love
and sometimes the things I love
break me.

Scars Are Made of Gold

They're scars for a reason.

They don't hurt anymore
but they're there to remind you
of all the things
you lived through.

The moments that almost
killed you
and the ones that made you
who you are.

Stay strong.

Broken People

I like broken people
with broken eyes and broken smiles.

I like people who feel too much
and have seen even more.

I like people who are silent
because they appreciate how sometimes
words can't explain the moment.

I like people who find themselves
in the most unusual places—where they go
to fall apart in solitude.

I admire these people,
I look up to these people,
and I appreciate these people,
for they know more about true love
than anyone else.

Grow in the Darkness

You have to allow yourself
to break apart.

That's the only way
you're going to know
what you're made of.

Let yourself go.

Let yourself fall.

Let yourself drown.

Let yourself shatter.

And above all,
let yourself get hurt.

Do all these things and know . . .

How you have to really know
your demons to defeat them.

Befriend them to destroy them.

Love them and walk with them.

That's the only way
you're going to bloom.

Why I Miss You, My Brother

Because the end of the world happens
at least once every hour
since you've been gone.

Because all the things I've told you
I've really meant.

Because without you there is no me.

Because it hurts
but I'm still breathing.

Because they say
"letting go" will "help me"
but all I could do is think about you.

Because I still love you
and you are not here.

Break me by the rocks and leave me there. Let me come back to you on the shore. Let me become all the seashells you were meant to collect.

It's No Longer Here

I cannot remember the ocean.

I live near it
and yet,
I cannot remember it.

It is not because I cannot go to it
but rather
because I choose to ignore it
because I know it is always there.

If I go far, the ocean stays.

If I die, the ocean stays
but somehow I cannot remember it.

The same way I cannot remember many
things, like things I used to do when I was a
kid.

Things that fed my soul.

I cannot remember things.

Sometimes I do not know myself.

Sometimes I cannot remember who I am.

The same way I cannot remember you.

I cannot.

Maybe this prose isn't making any sense
but that is not the point.

If you read this
and don't get it
then you just missed the point.

I cannot remember the ocean.

I cannot remember who I used to be.

Selective Programming

There are hidden truths in films,
music, and in stories.

Some truths cut deeper than others
and some truths are too ridiculous to even
consider.

There are hidden truths in media.

What you see is either fact or fiction
but most fiction is fact.

It is just buried from the population.

Fifty years before the moon landing, critics
and the people said it was impossible.

They made films about it, wrote music about
it, and even stories.

Now people walk on the moon.

Selective programming.

I want you to see things the way I see.

If I tell you man can fly it is because man
can fly.

I see it before it has happened.

If they tell you aliens exist it is because they
do and when they reveal themselves, you
will be okay with it.

Selective programming.

Here are the things that are on the media
now.

Wars, invasions, laser weapons, reptilians
gods, flying pyramids, and upside-down
crosses.

Kind of makes you want to think of all the
things you might see tomorrow.

Selective programming.

You were happy once. You were
cheerful and full of laughter.
That is how I want to remember
you. You are beautiful and I
miss you.

People Killer

The cops just killed an innocent man.

He wasn't doing anything wrong.

He was black and the cop was white.

I can't understand this racism thing.

This authority thing.

Cops are the law.

The law controls us all.

For every one cop there are ten thousand of us.

Cops can kill you for no reason
but you can go straight to jail, to hell, the
moment you kill, and for whatever reason.

Maybe someone broke into your house,
kidnapped your kid or even your mother.

You can't kill to protect yourself but a cop
can kill for pleasure.

I saw the cops kill an innocent man.

The video showed the man on the ground
surrendering.

It took five shots, the black man is dead.

The cop said he had a gun.

There was no gun.

When the people kill each other, it's your
word against theirs.

A cop kills a man and he's off the hook.

I saw a cop kill an innocent man.

His family mourns his death
while the cop sits at home and enjoys his
meal.

This Is My Space

What a suicide it is,
this social media stream.

This endless ocean of moments.

Once hooked it is over.

Once you are a member
it is as if you have signed
a life contract.

This prison.

This system.

This, this and that, that.

We all get on daily.

In the morning,
In the afternoon,
and in the very second
before we go to bed.

This social media thing is
in the blood.

It gives us life,
excitement,
and something to look forward to.

But what to do if no one stimulates you
anymore.

That is,
if no one replies or sends you messages.

What becomes of this social pool
if no appreciates you or comes looking for
you.

If no one cares about your moments,
your pictures, or even your videos.

What becomes of your social media if you
die. Does it die with you?

Perhaps it does, the same way
lovers die out into flame,
the one that no longer keeps us warm.

If there is no reaction then there is no action,
no purpose to keep it going.

It is the need of human interaction
that keeps us all online.

Somewhere in the vastness of the earth, there is a place where people go to, to laugh. Where sadness is not allowed and only love is shared. This place is quiet and empty. This place beats 70 times per minute and sound it makes is only for you. Come find me.

Dear Mother

Dear Mother,
if I die,
do not let me become a hashtag.

I am so much more than a few letters.

I am so much more than what I am.

Within me I have answers,
I have questions,
I have love,
and I have hatred.

All these twirl within me.

Aching my body for a sudden way out.

Dear Mother,
if I die,
do not let me become a hashtag.

Hashtags die down, they don't last.

They come and they go.

And I want to stay in people's hearts

the same way our childhood has stayed in
ours.

Dear Mother,
If I die,
do not let me become a hashtag.

I know there is more to people than sharing
terrible news and talking about how cops
have murdered innocent African Americans.

I know there is a light in everyone of us
and I know we all want change but do not
know how to touch change.

Dear Mother,
If I die,
just promise me this:

Do not let me become a hashtag.

There are so many other things I can
become.

I know it.

CPSIA information can be obtained
at www.ICGtesting.com
Printed in the USA
LVHW08s0622310718
585378LV00003B/525/P